TOP TIPS:
COMMUNICATING GOD IN
NON-BOOK WAYS

Kathryn Copsey and Jean Elliott

Copyright ©Scripture Union 2008
First published 2008, reprinted 2010
ISBN 978 1 84427 329 4

Scripture Union England and Wales
207–209 Queensway, Bletchley, Milton
Keynes, MK2 2EB, England
Email: info@scriptureunion.org.uk
Website: www.scriptureunion.org.uk

Scripture Union Australia, Locked Bag 2,
Central Coast Business Centre, NSW
2252
Website: www.scriptureunion.org.au

Scripture Union USA
PO Box 987, Valley Forge, PA 19482
Website: www.scriptureunion.org

The right of Kathryn Copsey and Jean
Elliott to be identified as authors of this
work has been asserted by them in
accordance with the Copyright, Designs
and Patents Act 1988.

British Library Cataloguing-in-Publication
Data: a catalogue record of this book is
available from the British Library.

Printed and bound in Singapore by
Tien Wah Press Ltd

Logo, cover design, internal design:
www.splash-design.co.uk

Internal illustrations: Colin Smithson

Typesetting: Richard Jefferson,
Author and Publisher Services

Adviser: Alison Hendy

Scripture Union is an international
Christian charity working with churches
in more than 130 countries, providing
resources to bring the good news about
Jesus Christ to children, young people
and families and to encourage them to
develop spiritually through the Bible and
prayer.

As well as our network of volunteers,
staff and associates who run holidays,
church-based events and school
Christian groups, we produce a wide
range of publications and support those
who use our resources through training
programmes.

Children matter facilitates cooperation
between all Christians who work with
children. For more details see
www.childrenmatter.net

CONTENTS

INTRODUCTION

The sun streams through the brightly coloured panes of the stained glass windows of the old church building – Jesus healing Jairus' daughter, Jesus and Peter walking on the water, Jesus with Mary and Martha, Jesus blessing the children, and the crucifixion are all depicted there in the glass. Pictures have long played an important part in communicating the Gospel.

The bread and wine of the communion service, the cross on the communion table, the simple fish shape found on lapels and car windows remind us that visual symbols have always been a part of proclaiming who Jesus is and what he's done.

Medieval mystery plays, the rediscovered paintings on the walls of cathedrals, Christian hymns, chants and songs through the ages, all remind us that although words are important, music, drama and pictures have always been part of telling the Christian story too.

Jesus himself was rarely without a visual aid:

"See how the lilies of the field grow."

"Throw your net on the right side!"

He stood a child in the centre of them.

He spat on the ground and made mud.

He borrowed a donkey.

The Holy Spirit settled on him like a dove.

We may now live in a post-literate, non-book culture, 'a world beyond words', but plenty of people have lived and followed Jesus in a non-book culture before. We are

Think about...
What are the differences between the 'non-book' culture that existed in Jesus' time and the 'non-book' culture that exists today?

simply rediscovering the richness of telling the Christian story in a variety of creative ways, as well as reading from the written page. Technology of course is the big difference in communicating in the 21st century – images, words and music speeding across the world and back in the blink of an eye; information at the touch of a button. Some adults are embracing this gladly and others, reluctantly, but this present generation of children and young people accept it as a normal part of the world they live in.

> **Think about...**
> 'Are we preparing our young to be pioneers in a world beyond words – or equipping them for a print age that for them no longer exists?' Gerard Kelly

It's not that reading isn't important any more, just that it's used in different ways. Story remains vitally important, but again, there was story long before there was reading and writing. Generations sat around camp fires together and shared their stories. Now, once more, story, or narrative, is replacing text. We can't resist a good story: something with human interest, something about a 'real' person. Maybe we'll watch *Big Brother*, maybe we'll read someone's blog, maybe we'll find out all we can about a celebrity or maybe we'll join an e-group to chat with others who share our interests. We're desperate for a connection, to relate to others, to develop real friendships with other people and with God. As children's and youth workers we need to help those in our care, who live in a world of celebrities, mobile phones, MP3 players, PSPs and *MySpace*, to make those friendships too.

Jesus, the Word, makes sense of everything. He became flesh and lived among us. God the Father knew it was time to communicate with his creation, in a very special way, the good news of his love and

forgiveness through relationship with us.
There is no other way.

Relationships involve the senses, the
emotions, words, pictures, music,
laughter, food and drink, song, dance,
drama, touch, listening, colour, sound,
silence, tears, time, movement and
stillness. They involve living life to the full.
We may live in a world beyond words, but
it makes no sense at all without the Word,
Jesus himself. This book is a celebration of
communicating Jesus in a multi-coloured kaleidoscope of ways.
We hope you enjoy it!

WHAT THE BIBLE HAS TO SAY

1

What does the Bible have to say about communicating the good news of our faith in non-book ways? Well actually nothing at all – and yet everything! We know, of course, that the individual books that came to form the Bible over several centuries and from different cultures emerged out of societies which were 'non-book'. It was the oral tradition that ensured that stories were passed from generation to generation by word of mouth. Eventually they were written down as a record of God dealing with his people in order that, for example, the eye-witness accounts of Jesus' ministry would not be forgotten.

But these are just the mechanics or the details of how we come to have this written record called the Bible. What the Bible itself has to say about *how* God communicates with us is much more far-reaching.

In God's image

Flooding through the whole Bible is the truth of Genesis 1:26 in which God creates people and says, 'Now we will make humans and they will be like us' (CEV). Each one of us as human beings, whether we acknowledge God or not, is made in God's image. Note that God is not saying 'my' image but 'our' image. It is the image of God in eternal relationship: Father, Son and Holy Spirit. In the same way, we are created to be in that richest of all places, in relationship with God and with each other. So from the moment of our creation, God's way of communicating with us is through relationship, through the loving, giving, enriching and empowering qualities of true friendship.

As we move on through the Old Testament we see this relational theme as God encounters his people again and again. He makes a covenant with Abraham that his children will be as many as the stars in the sky (Genesis 15:5). God challenges Moses to trust him completely at the burning bush (Exodus 3). God teaches David of his steadfast love and care (Psalm 23). God speaks to Isaiah, Jeremiah and Hosea of his love for his people, and his heartbreak at their unfaithfulness.

But God doesn't just leave it there. Alongside these very personal encounters, we see how God reinforces these relationships with concrete, practical illustrations. Animals, a smoking fire-pot and a torch cement God's covenant with Abraham. A bush that burns but is not consumed demonstrates God's holiness and power to Moses. Defeating a bear, a lion and a giant shows God's protection of David, and images of clay pots, pits, plumb lines and scales are used by the prophets.

The Old Testament is full of rich images and symbols that use all the senses: magnificent garments for the priests in blue, purple and red with gold thread; the sweet smell of incense; the pillar of fire by night and cloud by day and words as sweet as honey. Then there are victory shouts around the walls of Jericho, the wolf and the lamb lying down together, and images of God tearing the sky apart and riding on the wings of the wind.

The Word became flesh and blood

The gift of being in relationship with God who communicates with his people began in the Old Testament. It came to its fullness in the New Testament with the birth of a baby: God himself became a human being and came to live as one of us. As *The Message* puts it, 'The Word became flesh and blood and moved into the neighbourhood' (John 1:14). The Word who existed before the world was created, who spoke all life into being, who is above and beyond our imaginings and understandings, chose to take on flesh and blood and become like us in order to communicate his love with us. In doing this, God showed his favour and protection to humanity in a way which had never happened before.

As we look at Jesus' ministry, we see him building quality relationships with his disciples. He communicated very effectively with those around him: touching, looking, holding, loving, weeping, confronting, blessing, challenging. People responded to him. It was no one-way process. They ate with him (Luke 7:36), loved him in an extravagant way (Luke 7:44–47), and included him in their fishing exploits (Mark 4:38) and family crises (Mark 1:30–31).

Jesus, of course, was a great storyteller: 'There was a rich man…'; 'A farmer went out to sow his seed…'. Story captures a listener in a way no other media can as it invites us to bring our own experiences and feelings to the story, making it live for us. Whether telling parables, taking real-life examples, or reflecting on a scene before him, Jesus used ordinary, everyday objects and situations: a donkey in a pit, a coin, a busy vineyard owner, a traveller on his way to Jericho. No wonder he was able to make such good connections with his audience. These stories were then passed down from generation to generation. Long before they became universally available in written form, they were depicted in tapestries or in the stained glass windows of churches across the land: the poor man's Bible. City guilds performed them as mystery plays at festivals. Artists illustrated both the stories that Jesus told and the stories of his life.

In the life of the early church, we see the strong bonds of relationship continue. The believers were in close fellowship together, sharing their belongings, their money, their meals and their homes (Acts 2:43–47; 4:32–35). They were inspired by the stories of Jesus, their study of the Scriptures, and teaching that often used powerful imagery such as the unity of the body and treasure in clay pots. There were those of high status and education (Acts 17:12), including the apostle Paul, and others of low rank such as Onesimus, who was a runaway slave. Our knowledge of practices in the early church is limited, but baptism (Acts 2:41; 10:47–48) and the practice of celebrating the Lord's Supper (1 Corinthians 11:17–34) had become very visual symbols of the faith. The fish was one of the earliest symbols of Christian art because the letters of the Greek word for fish (ichthys) were an acronym for 'Jesus' (Iesous – Jesus Christ, the Son of God, Saviour).

SOME BASIC PRINCIPLES

2

The challenge to children's and youth work

If we are to communicate the Christian faith effectively to children in this post-print world, it is our responsibility to explore some non-book approaches. The year 1476 marked the beginning of the end of the non-book culture. William Caxton set up the first printing press in England and early in the 1500s, the first Bibles were printed. Although it was many years before every household could have access to or afford to own their own Bible, this invention ensured that books were here to stay.

We are now so used to the universal availability of books that we cannot imagine a world without them. Yet in the last ten to fifteen years, unlike the previous 500, a generation of non-readers has grown up in our society: it's not that they can't read, it's that they *choose* not to. Books are still read by some but the short snippets of reading matter to be found in magazines, newspapers, fanzines and comics are the preferred choice of reading matter for many. Surfing the net as both a work and leisure activity has become the key means of acquiring a knowledge of the world, superseding the radio and television. Podcasts are yet another means of acquiring information.

Instead of writing letters, communication is faster and more immediate by email, msn or chat rooms. Whether we like it or not, we are part of a generation that lives in a world beyond the written word, a world that in many ways is returning to the oral tradition where narrative and story again hold power.

How the church can respond

It seems that many Christians are apparently reluctant or even unable to accept that non-book approaches can be as valid as those which focus on text. (This is not to undermine the importance of the written text but to recognise that there are many ways to engage with it.) The unspoken message in many churches seems to be that non-book ways with their focus on affective learning (learning that comes through the senses and emotions) are a soft option we can adopt for little children, but once they get older the serious business of faith is tied up with words, books and cognitive learning or head knowledge.

Let's look at a typical traditional church. Enter the front door and you will be handed some combination of a hymnbook, a Bible, an order of service and a news-sheet. Go to sit down and you'll find yourself in a pew or on one of a row of chairs facing the front, reminiscent of schoolrooms as they used to be – all very different from the interactive groups in today's classroom. There's usually a lot to read in the service: hymns and songs (either from a book or perhaps from words projected onto a screen), perhaps a set liturgy from a service book, passages from the Bible, prayers. The sermon, address, reflection, or 'ministry of the word' (as it is called in some churches) usually takes the form of a monologue by the minister, vicar or priest, which the congregation listens to in silence. It is rarely interactive. It is doubtful whether anyone would experience this style of teaching in any other setting in their week. Children certainly would not.

In some churches there is the opportunity to exchange the peace with neighbours and through this to recognise that people present are a part of the family of God. The service of Holy Communion or Last

Supper, which may or may not include children, does allow for movement and participation, but it could be very easy for someone to enter, sit down, go through the entire service and leave at the end without speaking to anyone at all! Of

Think about…
Reflect on how bookshops and libraries have changed in the last twenty years. What motivated those changes? How have your church services changed in that time?

course, this is not always the case. Numerous churches provide interactive all-age services and café-style approaches, but the structure of many services actually discourages the building of relationships. A key biblical principle has been lost.

Most churches running groups for children offer a wide variety of imaginative activities and sessions, often with limited resources and facilities. Many churches, however, still refer to the children's activities using the language of school, for example, retaining the term Sunday 'school' with 'teaching' material used by 'teachers' who in their 'lessons' help the 'class' of children explore a Bible story, ending with completing a 'worksheet'! The children come from a wide variety of backgrounds, ages and abilities. It is a challenge to select activities that will connect with their different learning styles and needs. Some always seem to want to be active and have difficulty sitting still. Others don't seem to be able to concentrate and seem to be somewhere else. Still others are full of stories and chat that take the session off on a tangent, while some want to know every detail of who did what and when in the story! Some children really enjoy doing the wordsearch in the worksheet, some struggle to write well enough to fill in the blanks, some lose interest in it because it reminds them of school and fold it into a paper aeroplane, and some don't want to take it home.

If we only offer this book-based educational model, we are forced to ask how much worship and engagement with God occurred in our sessions and how much learning from relationship was ever allowed to emerge.

Health check on your Sunday children's and youth group

So, many of our church children's and youth groups have structures and approaches which are inextricably linked with the written word in its

> How long are the children/young people expected to sit and listen to the adults?
>
> How strictly do you keep to the 'lesson' for the day, even if the group wants to explore one aspect more fully?
>
> How do you use games to illustrate the theme or do you have doubts about the value of having fun with games?
>
> Do you avoid messy activities because clothes or the church hall carpet might get dirty?
>
> How concerned are you about what parents or others in the church think about your session? Do you have any accountability?
>
> Do you feel your session is incomplete unless there is a take-home worksheet, even if you have to fill it in for them?
>
> What songs do you sing? How meaningful are the words of these songs for the children? Are they expected to read the words?
>
> Are all your activities of one style or are you able to include time for movement, stillness, interaction and the creative arts?
>
> Think of each person in your group: what activities do they most enjoy and how will you cater for each one?
>
> God created us to grow through relationship. How far do you believe that building quality relationships in your session is the most important part of what you do?

many forms. Some of these structures actively discourage relationship-building which is so core to the way God communicates with us. It is good every now and again to measure the health of our activities. How would your leaders respond to the following questions?

It's fun to be alive

When did you last exchange the peace with another member of your fellowship, or simply stop and greet a friend in the street? What did you feel? What senses did you use? Did you really 'see' them? Did you look them in the eyes? Were you in a rush or did you take time to really take in the other person? Did you really touch them, make contact with them? Did you listen to what they said to you or only hear them superficially?

Between childhood and adulthood there is a significant reduction in how we use our senses. It is through smell, touch and sound that a baby first begins to learn about the world around her, recognising mother through her smell, noting facial expressions and tones of voice long before she can understand words. Look how children will smell a new pair of shoes or mum's hair. They can't resist touching fresh paint or listening to interesting sounds like a buzzing fly. But as we grow older, all sorts of inhibitions and taboos creep in. A teenager is less likely than a five-year-old to sniff something to find out about it. Adults probably won't stare at someone who looks a little different, nor will they stop to listen to birdsongs but only hear them in the background.

Children learn through using their whole body, through using all their senses. Look at all the learning that takes place even before a child can read – before 'word' becomes all-important. Much of children's learning is 'affective' learning or learning through the use of their senses and emotions; learning which is intuitive and at a feeling level, rather than learning which is cognitive learning or head knowledge. Consider these figures:

A child remembers 10% of what she hears
50% of what she sees
60% of what she says
90% of what she does

No wonder it is important to explore creative ways of communicating our faith with children! We ourselves need to 'become like a child', making the Word come alive in ways that are not dependent on text. We can start with Jesus as our example: 'Jesus confronts us with the word that can be seen, heard and touched' (Nouwen). Jesus touched the woman with the bent spine. He spat and made mud to smear on the eyes of the blind man. He made a whip which he used to create havoc in the temple. He saved the day by providing the best wine for the wedding and when Thomas had trouble believing, Jesus invited him to touch and to look.

The old children's hymn begins, 'Tell me the stories of Jesus, I love to hear'. Communicating our faith in non-book ways is about exploring again how to communicate 'the story' so that it can come alive for our children and young people.

WHERE DO WE START? SOME PRACTICAL IDEAS

3

Communicating through relationship

God is a God of relationship. We need to be reminded of this again and again. He himself is in relationship – the relationship of the Trinity: Father, Son and Holy Spirit. He made people to be in relationship with him and with one another. We live in a world crying out for good and positive relationships but in many cases people have forgotten how to make them. Children are looking for positive role models and turning more and more to celebrities to provide these.

It is impossible to overemphasise the importance of growing good relationships with the young people in our groups and clubs. It speaks volumes, just being there for them week after week, calling them by name, remembering their favourite football teams, being prepared to chat with them, listen to them, play a game with them or have fun with them. How about planning a special treat or outing? How much of yourself do you share with them? What jokes do you share? If the children get to know you, and Christ is in you, then the children will see Jesus!

The Christian story is about relationship. It *is* relationship – it's about love and forgiveness, enjoying being in God's company, getting to know him better and better, and loving and forgiving the people he's made. Never forget that spending TIME with children is communicating more than we can know.

In reality…
On a midweek-club weekend away, Jake stood at the top of the hill we had climbed and said, "Wow! Look at the view! This is the best weekend of my life!"

Jesus chose to come and spend time being 'one of us' so that we can be in relationship with him for ever. That's something to communicate!

Communicating through pictures and symbols

Pictures are powerful communication tools. People communicated through pictures long before the written word was developed. There is a long history of telling Bible stories with pictures: flannelgraphs, large drawings, overhead projector acetates and now, PowerPoint. Pictures give a focus and a sequence. There don't need to be too many but they do need to be big and eye-catching enough to hold children's attention. They could be of characters from the story drawn 'seaside pier-style' on sheets of card with apertures for the children to put their heads through; on rolls of lining paper, gradually unfurled; on large sheets of card pegged up in sequence on a 'washing line'; built up like a jigsaw puzzle or layered so that pieces can be added or taken off using Blu-tack or Velcro. They could be photographs, or a collage of images cut out from magazines or downloaded from the Internet. They could be all sorts of objects that tell a story or communicate something about the God we want the children to discover, something the children can touch, feel or smell.

In her book, *Stories, Stories Everywhere*, Sandra Pollerman describes the use of story-cloths which incorporate many stories in one picture. She also gives a brief introduction to *Godly Play*, a way of helping children engage with the Christian story through symbols, simple wooden figures and story mats, asking questions to encourage reflection and then inviting a creative response. This method was developed by Jerome Berryman. For more details see page 31

Communicating through technology

Technology, in all its forms, continues to develop. It is well worth thinking about how you can use it creatively with the children you work with. For a small group a television or computer screen is fine, but for a larger group, a large screen and data projector are invaluable. Reflections with images, words and music can be produced; film clips can be shown; videos can be made of your group acting out Bible stories. Digital cameras can be used to tell stories in a series of 'still' pictures; or to produce a series of photos to illustrate a psalm. The Internet, of course, offers all kinds of pictures and materials for you to use, including the Lego series of Bible stories!

Young people and many children, of course, communicate through their mobile phones or on MSN or by

> **In reality...**
> A children's house group videoed the Big Story of the Bible in ten short scenes and showed it in a service of all-age worship.

joining a social network such as Bebo or MySpace. Images, music and ideas are passed round these networks as people build relationships. This opens up huge opportunities for those engaged in children's and youth ministry. Needs for prayer and answers to prayer are made immediately available. Spiritual insights, enthusiastic interest in God, doubts and uncertainties are given an airing. Making God and his story known through modern technology has never been easier! For more details see Connect series: *The iPod* (see page 31 for details).

We also need to be aware of the potential dangers of such new technology. The Churches Child Protection Advisory Service (CCPAS) produces some very helpful booklets for both adults and young people, such as *Help me chat safely...on the net, when I email, on my mobile'* (see page 32 for details).

Communicating through food and hospitality

There are an amazing number of meals described in the Bible. Small groups of people such as Peter's mum-in-law, Martha and Mary and Zacchaeus welcomed Jesus into their homes. There are stories of great banquets, wedding feasts and huge picnics and the very special supper Jesus had with his friends. Food communicates and draws people together and children love food! (Do check for food allergies though.) What's more, children can help prepare food themselves. All this helps to build relationships.

Find food to illustrate a theme. Introduce the sorts of food Jesus might have eaten when talking about his visit to the home of Zacchaeus – figs, pitta bread, grape juice, watermelon, oranges, hummus. Bread can be baked when thinking about a variety of Bible passages. Chocolate Angel Delight makes great mud for the eyes of the blind man Jesus healed. A delicious fruit salad goes down well when thinking about the Garden of Eden or the fruit of the Spirit. The possibilities are literally endless. Enjoy!

> **In reality…**
> Some teenagers made the most wonderful non-alcoholic cocktails in a retelling of the wedding at Cana.

Communicating through music and sound

Music plays an integral part in our daily lives. We hear it on the radio, in shops, in lifts, on the TV, at sporting events, in church and some even sing in the shower! It also contributes to the development of our spiritual lives. David's harp playing soothed King Saul; we are encouraged in the Psalms to praise God with all instruments and to sing a new song; the book of Revelation gives us a glimpse of worship in heaven. We can listen to music together: attending a concert, or listening to musical extracts can provide a way in to discussion on a Bible passage or Biblical truth; it might be the stimulus for a piece of creativity, meditation or prayer. Or it might just provide the space needed to spend time alone with God, reflecting on his wonderful word. Don't limit your musical range: music by *Planetshakers, T-Bone or Delirious?* may not touch you but may connect with your young people.

We can sing: corporate singing is an extremely spiritual experience, and can range from Taizé chants to Matt Redman choruses, Gospel songs and spirituals to U2 numbers. There are plenty of CDs available of worship songs for children (including SU's *Reach Up* and *Light for Everyone*) and there are, of course, 'adult' worship songs which are appropriate for children too. It's worth selecting carefully to find the right songs for your group, which they enjoy singing. Include quieter songs as well as lively ones and try using song in prayer times to encourage the children to listen to God. Avoid songs which include words and concepts the children are unlikely to understand or relate to. Percussion instruments, sign language and actions can all enrich singing and can encourage children to worship with their whole bodies. This also means they can minister to each other, too.

Music can be used to communicate Bible stories and passages. It can be used in the background, eg *Morning* from *Peer Gynt* in the story of creation, or *Fossils* from *Carnival of the Animals* in the telling of Ezekiel and the dry bones. Of course, there are endless possibilities all through the Bible for using percussion as sound effects – the walls of Jericho, the calming of the storm, the crucifixion, the resurrection and Pentecost. There is scope for composing too. Try using voices, unusual instruments or body percussion where percussive sounds are made using bodily movements such as clapping, whistling, stamping, or tapping thighs and chest. Have a go at sound collage that uses portions or samples of existing songs mixed together in a different order. You could retell an entire story or focus on certain themes, concepts or emotions. You could use contrasting pieces of music for storm and peace, dark and light, death and life, for example.

Don't forget that children enjoy making their own instruments. Those whose instrument performance skills are more developed could be involved in a worship group. Ruth Wills' book, *Everyone's a Winner*, has a useful section on music games as well as hints and tips for using music as a method of Bible teaching (see page 31 for details).

Communicating through all the senses

Smell the fresh hay combined with the steamy smell of the animals; touch the baby's soft cheek and downy head, the roughness of the donkey's back; hear the quiet clucking of the hens, the snoring of the ox; see the outline of the manger as your eyes grow accustomed to the candlelight, the smile on Mary's face, the concern on Joseph's; taste the crusty bread and spicy soup which has just arrived from the inn-keeper…

Every Bible passage is full of opportunities for using the senses. Not every sense has to be used every time, of course, but be aware of how different senses can be engaged with different passages. You might fill the room with a beautiful smell when telling the story of the woman who poured perfume on Jesus' feet; listen to the sounds the deaf man may have heard when Jesus unstopped his ears, or touch different fabrics and think what the woman who touched Jesus' cloak may have felt. You could taste the breakfast on the beach that Jesus ate with his friends or describe something beautiful like a flower as the blind man who could see again might have described it.

Many children enjoy the opportunity to dress up and be involved in the impromptu acting out of a Bible story. Look out for passages which lend themselves to this and enjoy really 'getting into' a story. Young people's creativity and inventiveness should be stimulated in using drama and the senses to bring stories alive.

Communicating through storytelling

Everyone loves a good story. Jesus knew this and could pack a story full of colour and meaning into a few sentences. As we've already seen, pictures, symbols, technology, food, music and the senses can all be

used in story-telling, but there are times when it may be appropriate for someone simply to tell a cracking good story! Maybe a simple prop will be used; maybe the storyteller will be dressed as a character; maybe there'll be a phrase for the listeners to repeat from time to time, or sound effects for them to make, or maybe there will just be the story, the storyteller, the listeners – and God! The storyteller needs to be sure of their story: of the shape of it and where it's going; of the rhythm of it and whether there will be a repeated phrase to help the listeners keep tuned in; of whether there will be surprises; of the tone and volume of their voice and of the mood and reaction of the listeners. The story shouldn't go on for too long. 'Leave them wanting more' has always been the adage here. Storytelling still works – try it!

For more details read *Top Tips on Sharing Bible stories* – see page 33.

Communicating through art

God delighted in making an amazing world full of life, colour, pattern, texture and variety and bursting with creativity. He made people in his own image and so we're creative too. That's exciting, but some children, especially as they grow older, seem to have few opportunities to be creative. This means that although they may be lacking in confidence they generally love the chance to paint or stick something, especially if it involves glitter and sparkly bits! Creating something in response to, or for use in, a Bible story or passage then, is often very welcome. Art is much more than colouring something in or sticking A to B to make a pre-described model (although there's occasionally a place for this). It's an opportunity to make a unique response to God and can be an act of worship to God in itself. Art and craft materials are widely available in high street shops and through mail order. It is helpful to have a basic stock of paper of different sizes, ready-mix paints, glue, scissors, felt-tip pens and collage materials always at hand.

Using other people's art and 'famous' paintings can be a useful starting point. For example, comparing two artists' interpretations of the Good Samaritan gives a springboard for a child's own collage/drawing/model of how they want to interpret that story. The Internet gives access to thousands of works of art and the Stapleford Centre produces special packs (see page 32 for details).

In reality...
Scott, a nine-year-old who appeared at our mid-week club, was amazed that we 'talked to God', a totally new concept to him. Nevertheless, he clung tightly to the pipe-cleaner figure someone helped him to make to remind him how special he was to God.

Communicating through nature

The whole of nature communicates God and his amazing creativity! It's important to give those in our groups and clubs opportunities to experience God's creation first-hand. They may have many opportunities to do this without you, or they may not. It's a very special experience to take children who've never seen the sea before for a day at the seaside! A trip to a local park, nature reserve or urban farm can be just as worthwhile, as can a walk around a local area. So many children and young people walk round with their eyes blinkered and often with earplugs in their ears. Encourage their powers of observation! A walk

on a clear night away from city street lights can be an awe-inspiring experience for anyone who rarely has the opportunity to see the star-spangled heavens – and who never experiences real darkness! Give time to stop and listen – and to wonder.

In reality…

From my window, as I write, I can see part of a churchyard and at least seven types of trees and plants and a beautiful spider's web. I can hear several birds and the clouds in the sky are magnificent – all this in East London.

Communicating through games

We know that many children spend huge periods of time playing games on screens of one kind or another, and much has been written about how this may affect them socially, but the good news is this – children still enjoy what might be called good old traditional games such as 'Duck, duck, goose', 'Simon says', 'Stick in the mud', 'Chocolate dice', 'Dodge ball', 'Port and starboard', team games, wide games and hundreds of others. There are many good games books on the market (see resources list on page 31), including some containing games which are themed to be used with particular Bible stories or to communicate a Christian value in a fun way. When playing games, think about what's appropriate for the age-group of the children. Avoid games in which children are 'out' for any length of time. Play canopies (parachutes) are very popular and are great for encouraging cooperative play as well as being lots of fun. Play canopies can also be used in communicating Bible stories (especially those involving storms and water) and are excellent for interpreting Psalms visually using different movements for each phrase.

Communicating through the Bible itself

We've looked at many examples of how we can communicate the message of the Bible in non-book ways, but it is important that children have opportunities to handle a Bible for themselves. The content of the Bible is like a treasure which we can take out, look at and explore piece by piece. But sometimes it is good to see it in the context of the whole treasure chest. Children who do not have a Bible of their own are often excited by the numbers of pages, the thinness of the paper, and the fact that one of the books may bear their name or that of one of their friends. Even less fluent readers can be happy to read a verse from the Bible if they are part of a small group where they feel accepted and valued. While no one should ever be *made* to read aloud from the Bible, the opportunity should be there. Children need to be able to see where the stories and passages which help us to get to know God actually come from.

When choosing a set of Bibles for your group, make sure the print is clear and of a good size and that the translation is one which is easily accessible to children. The Contemporary English Version (CEV) and the New Century Translation are especially clear. A very accessible new version is the NIrV Bible (Narrative and Illustrated) where the main story flows simply through the pages while the sub-text (genealogies, letters, laws, etc) is set in double columns. For a younger group, a recently published children's 'Bible' with up-to-date illustrations provides the context for the stories with which the children are engaging. Enjoy choosing one which is right for your particular group.

Think through...

The story of Mary Jones, the Welsh girl who walked miles to buy her very own Bible made a big impression on me when I was a child. What stories or examples from your life will you pass onto children that might have a similar impact?

All people, whatever their age, can encounter God as they hear the Bible read aloud. The Contemporary English Version was deliberately phrased to be listened to rather than read. Of course, this means that readers need to read well, having prepared their passage, introducing it clearly and suggesting clues to help listeners follow the story or theme. Suggestions for sound effects and props are given on pages 21–22.

In reality…
8- to 11-year-olds who certainly weren't regarded as 'good readers' at school, loved to read the Bible aloud at their mid-week club where they evidently felt secure and valued.

TEN TOP TIPS

1. Think relationships

2. Think visual

3. Involve all the senses

4. Offer choices

5. Be creative!

6. Don't assume children don't want to read the Bible

7. Think low-tech as well as high-tech

8. Be aware of ways children communicate

9. Be aware of different learning styles

10. Keep things moving but make time for stillness

RESOURCES

Resource books

Sandra Pollerman, *Stories, Stories Everywhere*, BRF, 2001

Jerome W. Berryman, *Godly Play*, Augsburg Press, 1991

Jerome W. Berryman, *The Complete Guide to Godly Play*, Living the Good News, 2002

Ruth Wills, *Everyone's a Winner*, Scripture Union, 2001

Sue Wallace, *Multi-sensory Church* (and the rest of this series), SU, 2002

Xpedition Force (holiday club material using the senses), SU, 2003

Lesley Pinchbeck, *Theme Games 2*, SU, 2002

Lesley and Neil Pinchbeck, *Zoe and Zac's Blue and Red Games Kits*, CURBS, 2001

One Day Wonders, CURBS, 2008

The Big Picnic, CURBS, 2007

Brian Draper, *Connect series: The iPod*, SU, 2007

Keepin' it Real: exploring choices with 9-13 year olds, Methodist Church & CURBS, 2007

Lucy Moore, *Messy Church*, BRF, 2006

Kathryn Copsey, *From the Ground Up*, BRF, 2005

Bob Hartman, *Telling the Bible*, Monarch, 2006

Lesley Wright, *Bible Food Fun*, Dorling Kindersley, 2000

Scripture Union's curriculum material, *Light* encourages multi-sensory engagement with God. All-Age Service Annual (SU) Vol 1 2007, Vol 2 2008

Storybooks for children

Robert Harrison, *The Strong Tower*, SU, 2006 (for 5 to 11s)

Big Bible Storybook, SU, 2007 (for under 8s)

Heather Butler, *The 10 Must know stories – Tales you just have to read*, SU, 2008 (for 8 to 11s)

Alexander Brown, *The Green Must know stories – Tales you just have to hear*, SU, 2008 (for under 8s)
Alexander Brown, *The Red Must know stories – Tales you just have to hear*, SU, 2008 (for under 8s)
Into the Bible: 101 routes to explore, SU, 2007 (for 5 to 11s)
Bob Hartman, *The Lion Storyteller Bible*, Lion Hudson 2001
Rhana Davies, *The Barnabas Children's Bible*, BRF, 2007

Websites

Baker Ross Craft Supplies, www.bakerross.co.uk 0870 458 5440
Seamstress Ltd. (playchutes), www.playchutes.com 01327 263933
The Stapleford Centre, www.stapleford-centre.org 0115 939 6270
CURBS, www.curbsproject.org.uk
The Churches Child Protection Advisory Service (CCPAS), www.ccpas.co.uk 0845 120 45 50
Godly Play, www.godlyplay.org.uk